Surviving Life

Surviving Life

J. Taylor

AuthorHouse ™
1663 Liberty Drive
Bloomington, IN 47403
www.authorhouse.com
Phone: 1-800-839-8640

Published by AuthorHouse   10/18/2012

ISBN: 978-1-4772-8280-9 (sc)
ISBN: 978-1-4772-8281-6 (e)

This book is dedicated to all of the children
that have been declared a ward of the state
and have shared this nightmare to one
extent or another and survived!

CONTENTS

FOREWORD

INTRODUCTION TO SURVIVING LIFE

The story you are about to read is true; it is often been said that to truly find out who you are you have to remember where you came from. In some cases where you came from allows you to discover what you are capable of achieving, and surviving, in my case that is true, not always good but true. I was abandoned at birth, adopted, orphaned at 14, homeless living on the streets of Chicago at 14 as a runaway from a foster home, committed to the Chicago State Hospital at 14, escaped from the Chicago State Hospital at 16, hitchhiked all over the United States, working day labor and staying in homeless shelters to survive, joined the United States Navy with a fake ID at 17, discharged after boot camp for being under age, joined the Illinois National Guard at 19 and was discharged for insubordination, re-joined the United States Navy at 21 volunteered for the Submarine Service and served four years aboard two nuclear submarines.

After receiving a Honorable Discharge in 1980, I got married had three wonderful children, like everything else in my life that was not sustainable and ended abruptly. I have spent most of my life going from job to job, in and out of alcohol treatment programs and mental health facilities. I have never been able to maintain any level of stability. I am currently 58 years old and possess an 8th grade education. The following psychological report was written at the Chicago State Hospital when I was 16 years old:

BEHAVIOR DURING EVALUATION

Jessie is a lanky boy of fair complexion. He begins the examination by saying it should be easy since he can do work at the college level. His performance does not justify this contention. Even after he demonstrated to himself that he is not as smart as he wishes others to believe, he continues with his grandiose statements. In the Rorschach he states that he could see "a million things in the blot" yet he could only give a 'one or two responses to each card and sees nothing in card VII. In the TAT he says "I am a writer so that's no problem." His stories, however instead of revealing originality are rather stereotyped and sterile. The boy expresses a conception of himself that does not coincide with objective reality. Apparently, he is attempting to compensate for feelings of intellectual inadequacy. Such feelings are realistic in light of his performance. Another interesting detail deals with his continuous attempts to cheat. Attaining a high score and thus appearing to be bright is so important to him that he is willing to get it by underhanded means. In picture completion, for instance, he attempts to read the answers from the test booklet, it is difficult for him to read upside down, but he tries hard anyway, he is constantly watching me and checking my handwriting, to see what I am writing. The first impression is that the boy is giving to bragging that he is suspicious, and that he may be dishonest.

INTELLECTUAL FUNCTIONING

Jessie shows severe inefficiencies in his intellection organization. He obtains an IQ of 81, dull normal, in the WAIS, but he does not function in an integrated fashion even at this limited level. His verbal competence allows him to achieve an average IQ of (94) when the task requires manipulation of verbal symbols; his difficulties with perceptual-motor organization allow him to reach only the level of mild mental retardation (IQ 66) in psycho-motor tasks. This large discrepancy (28 points) as well as marked scatter of his scores (from 2 to 1) suggests some form of encephalopathy. There are strong indications, of organic involvement affecting primarily cognitive areas involved in visual-motor perception. Knowing nothing about this boy other than his birth date, it is difficult to give a clear picture of the cause of his condition. One would like to know the results of previous testing, his obtained grade placements of 11.2, 5.1, and 4.4 in reading, spelling, and arithmetic, receptively with an IQ of 81, a boy his age is expected to achieve at the 5.9-6.0 grade level. The fluctuations and discrepancies are outstanding. It might well be that he might have a minimal brain dysfunction aggravated by recent drug abuse. There is also the possibility of a tumor or some other disease process affecting the brain. It is necessary to follow through on these leads in order to reach an accurate diagnosis. The impairment of cognitive ability is evident. The suggestion of deterioration is very strong. The probability of impulsive, uncontrolled, antisocial behavior is overwhelming.

In Relationships outside of the family setting, Jessie shows difficulties in social contacts. He is overly preoccupied with himself, self-centered, and shows a lack of regard for the feelings and interest of others. His heterosexual relations are apt to end in failure. He feels so dejected, so insignificant, that he may gain power and status and thus feelings of status and satisfaction only from acting out. His antisocial behavior may bring him in trouble with the law.

DIAGNOSTIC IMPRESSION

Organic brain syndrome with psychotic features and antisocial behavior in the form of drug abuse, runaway, thievery, etc.

SUMMARY

Jessie attempts to present himself as an effective alert bright young man who is in possession and control of outstanding intellectual functions. He comes through however, as a bragging dishonest, suspicious boy over-whelmed by the feelings of insufficiency and inadequacy. This is ample evidence for both organic and psychotic thought disorder. In addition, his impulsivity and uncontrolled acting out suggest antisocial features in his character makeup which may bring him trouble with the law. His emotional conflicts are severe but difficult to disentangle from the effects of the presumed organic.

March 11, 2008

Jessie Taylor
10015 N. 9th Street
Tampa, Florida 33612

Dear Mr. Taylor:

I have received your letter of February 15, 2008. As I read your letter, I am deeply saddened and dismayed by the experiences you encountered as a young child. I cannot imagine the difficulties that you faced at every juncture, and how these situations may have impacted your adult life. I can only apologize to you for the insensitivity of the entire system at that time, and the manner is which that administration attempted to identify solutions to meet your needs.

As the Department of Human Services reflects on the journey that this service system has come over the past thirty years, we are keenly aware that in the 1960s, 1970s, and unfortunately 1980s, the collective systems were not always sensitive to the needs of the population that we were charged to serve. We recognize that many of the practices employed, at that time, to address the needs of children and adolescents did not take into account best practice models of care for children separate from that offered to adults. We also recognize that those in charge approached service delivery from a totally different perspective, which current wisdom would neither condone nor replicate.

I can emphatically state that children and adolescent consumers of services under the auspices of the Illinois Department of Human Services are treated with compassion, dignity and respect. As I reflect on the content of your letter, I can identify where many gaps occurred in not ensuring your rights, and subjecting you to these untenable situations.

I hope that you are now receiving appropriate support services in your home state. If not, I encourage you to seek support from the local mental health center in Tampa.

Sincerely,

Lorrie Rickman Jones, Ph.D.
Director of Mental Health

CHAPTER ONE

The Beginning

Everyone at some point and time in their life looks back retrospectively, and believes that if this had happened or that had happened, or if they had done this or done that, or made better decisions in many different situations, that their lives would have been better and they would have achieved greater success in either their personal lives or their professional lives. These same thoughts have led me to the brink of destruction at different points in my life. My story is of survival from a very young age, I was adopted at birth, orphaned at 14, lived on the streets of Chicago alone for three months at 14, placed in a juvenile correctional facility, and committed to the infamous Chicago State Hospital at 15, first into the men's receiving unit and then to a children's ward, hitchhiked around the country for a year and a half when I was 16 & 17, Joined the United States Navy at 17 after being picked up by a Navy Recruiter while I was hitchhiking, kicked out of the Navy after boot camp, for being underage at 17, kicked out of the Army National Guard at 19 for insubordination, rejoined the Navy at 21 and went on to serve in the United States Navy Submarine Service for four years aboard two nuclear submarines.

According to birth records I was born on October 7, 1954 with the name Clacy Powell I was immediately placed up for adoption, I was then adopted by Jessie and Francis Taylor from New York and given the name Jessie Taylor Jr. My earliest memories place me in the small town of Earle, Arkansas where my Father owned a little restaurant apparently that did not last long because he took out a loan from the local bank and on the way out of town congratulated them on being the new owners of his business. From there we moved to West Helena, Arkansas where we rented a small duplex apartment with a back yard, my father got a job driving a candy truck for "TOMS" I can still remember him coming home for lunch and letting me go in the truck and pick out a piece of candy.

Not long after we arrived in West Helena my parents bought a house at 301 North 2nd Street. This was the most wonderful place in the world with a large front yard and a little family owned grocery store next door. I loved this place it was a child's paradise a huge front yard with a tree for climbing, a picnic table, and a brick BBQ pit that my dad had built. My Father got a new job and began working at a gas station that was walking distance from the house. In 1959 I began 1st grade at Beech Crest School back then the teachers were allowed to spank you but my teacher had a different system she would call you to the front of the class and tell you to put your hands out palm up and smack them with a wooden ruler, then you would have to go into the coat room and face the wall until she told you that you could come out. One time she smacked my hands so hard they blistered and swelled up and my mom very angry. My dad went to the school and confronted them, well the teacher was allowed to finish the school year and then she resigned, but on her way out she flunked me and I had to do the first grade all over again the following year which was pretty much uneventful and I moved on to the second grade and Mrs. Lee's classroom.

Mrs. Lee was and still is my favorite teacher she was kind and caring and was born to be a teacher; she was not only our teacher but also our friend. I learned more in the short time I was in her class than I had learned in my previous two years at Beech Crest, but I did not know about the storm that was brewing on the horizon, and we were about to move again. Some of my fondest memories of West Helena were of the Little Girl that lived across the street her name was Lisa she was in my class at school and we were best friends one time we got caught playing doctor in her room and that created a little tension between our parents but we remained best friends. My mom worked nights at a clothing store in Helena, Arkansas which was about a mile from West Helena around a hill with a Hospital on top of it, (Helena was the County Seat for Phillips County) at night when she got off of work I would go with my dad in our 1960 Ford Falcon to pick her up three nights a week. We would always stop at "TASTEE FREEZE" on the way home for ice cream. I remember Christmas of 1961 I was so excited as I always was on Christmas Eve waiting for Santa Clause to see what he would bring me, my mom was in the kitchen cooking and she needed something from the store so me and my dad got in the car and went to Kroger, when we returned lo and behold Santa Clause had come and gone and my mom swore that she didn't hear a thing, but I had got everything that I asked for so I was a happy camper.

My mom was suffering from Emphysema and being a chain smoker was not helping her condition and my dad did not have medical insurance from his job at the gas station, he did have an old friend in Chicago that offered to get him a Union Job as a machinist at Burney Brothers Bakery this job would pay double what he was currently making and have full benefits so needless to say we sold the house and everything we owned and packed up the Ford Falcon and left for Chicago, leaving behind West Helena, Mrs. Lee, Beech Crest School and Lisa I was very sad. I still remember when I told Mrs. Lee that we were moving to Chicago, she replied "why would anyone want to move to Chicago?".

CHAPTER TWO

———⊶∞∞⊷———

Welcome To Chicago

We arrived in Chicago in our 1960 Ford Falcon me my dad and my mom, and everything we owned packed inside, looking like the Beverly Hillbilly's coming to town. We rented a single room in a rooming house on the southwest side of town and my mom enrolled me in the nearest Chicago Public School, where I became a circus attraction because of my southern accent I never made any friends at this school but I was only there for a short time. Not long after we arrived in Chicago my dad got good news and bad news he was going to get the job that he came for but he was going to have to wait for an opening, so he found a job at a Clark gas station just outside of Chicago in the suburb of Summit, Illinois, and we rented an apartment on the far south side close to the gas station, it was a very nice place to live but it was a concrete jungle with no place to play other than the side walk out front, I did make a few friends while we lived here and I wrote to Mrs. Lee and my old class in West Helena and to my pleasure they wrote back. In February of 1963 my father's job at Burney Brothers Bakery came through and we moved to the Austin District neighborhood on the West side of Chicago which was where the bakery was located.

The Austin neighborhood was a wonderful place to grow up at the time, we had moved into a small apartment in a large apartment building there were lots of kids in the area our apartment had a large room with a pull down double bed that was concealed behind two doors on the wall, and a walk in closet which became my room, a small dining room with French doors, and a small kitchen. It was a three story building and we were on the second floor our window was on the alley side we were the last apartment at the end of the hallway, halfway down the hallway going toward the front of the building on the right hand side was a small metal door with a handle on the center of the wall this was the garbage chute, it was an incinerator and when you opened the door sparks would sometimes fly out into the hallway, for a kid this was very cool stuff. My mom enrolled me in Henry Nash Elementary School which was a very good school and I made a lot of friends, my best friend was a kid named Bill he had two brothers and a sister he was a year older than me we went to the same school and lived in the same building as we did, his dad was a truck driver and his mom was not only the Avon lady but was also the buildings hairdresser and my mom became close friends with her. Summer came and school was out and I spent the summer exploring the neighborhood and making new friends and created a few enemies too. Every Sunday I would get dressed in my suit and go to church with Bill and his family it was a Lutheran Church and my mom liked this and talked my dad into enrolling me into the Christ Lutheran School next to the church, my dad was against this but whatever my mom wanted he did I have never seen two people that loved each other as much as they did. When school started in the fall I was no longer enrolled at Nash and now I had to walk three blocks to the soda fountain and wait for a bus to take me to my new school, each morning and I had to wear a shirt and tie every day and I was pissed I wanted to return to Nash where all of my friends were.

By November of 1963 my mother's health situation had become very serious, and on her bad days I would stay home from school so she wouldn't be alone, one such day was the day President Kennedy was assassinated

I watched that happen on our little black and white portable TV as my mother lay in the bed behind me, all of the employers in Chicago and around the country let their employees go home, and all of the women in the building were crying upon hearing of the President's death, it was truly a very sad day for the entire nation. About a week before Christmas my mom had become so ill that she had to go to the hospital and I went to stay with Bill and his family because my dad stayed at the Hospital around the clock with my mom. Christmas Morning of 1963 I was nine years old and I saw my dad for the first time in a week he came to Bills house and picked me up and we went home when we got there everything I had asked Santa for was under the Christmas tree, and then my Dad started crying and told me that my mother had passed away last night and was now in Heaven. Later that night he got drunk and never sobered up again. My dad went all out for the funeral, Bronze casket, formal gown etc. it took him three years to pay it off.

The next five years was kind of rough my father stayed drunk most of the time, he only sobered up to go to work. I got kicked out of Christ Lutheran School for not meeting their dress code so I returned to Nash where my friends were, I was pretty happy about that. My father had begun bringing women home from the bar and calling them our new housekeeper the first two were terrible but the third one Florence was nice and she moved in with us even though she was a drunk I liked her, and then we moved to a two bedroom basement apartment across the street and that placed me into a different school district. I had to transfer again from Nash to John Hayes Elementary School for the three years that we lived there, I now had a very long walk to school each day and I hated it. Soon after we moved my friend Bill's parents had bought a home on the south side and they moved out of the neighborhood, but they would come back to visit from time to time, I looked forward to those visits.

I had made a lot of friends in the neighborhood and was having a great time, by the 6th grade I had become a businessman. I went into the shoeshine business. I broke up an old wooden produce crate from behind the Jewel Grocery Store and built a shoe shine box, then I got my dad to invest in my business my removing enough money from his wallet while he was passed out drunk to buy the supplies that I needed (he blamed Florence for the missing money, I still feel bad about that), then I went to all of the bars and charged a quarter for a shoeshine and I was making a lot of money. We had moved to a second floor Apartment on the corner of Chicago Ave and Cicero by this time across the street from the J&B Snack shop where I used most of my earnings to buy my meals since no meals were being cooked at home just lots of drinking there. I was also back at Nash Elementary School which is where I wanted to be. I also started smoking Cigarettes around this time. The shoe shine business was very competitive and there were other kids doing this too. I claimed all of the bars on Chicago Ave. If I saw any one else with a shoe shine box I would kick their ass and destroy their shoe shine box, or keep it if it was nicer than mine until one day someone put a rock upside my head from the other side of the street and knocked me out (to this day I still have a knot on my forehead from that). This experience made me re-think the shoeshine business, so I got into the newspaper business much safer.

I found out from the guy that owned the newsstand on the corner that every evening the newsstands were staffed by the Chicago Tribune. I was told that if I went down to the

Tribune Loading Dock in the Afternoon they would maybe give me a news stand to work each evening. After school the following day I went down to the loading docks at the Chicago Tribune building on lower Wacker Drive. There were a bunch of bums sitting on stacks of newspapers some of them smelled pretty bad and they all smelled of cheap wine, the Tribune provided free coffee and donuts for them while they were waiting to be taken to their newsstands, after talking with a few of them I found out who to see to get a News Stand. I walked into the circulation office and gave my sales pitch and they looked at me like I was crazy, I was just a kid but I convinced them to give me a shot and they did, they sent me to the news stand at Madison & Wabash in downtown Chicago.

The way it worked was the Newspaper Drivers would advance you a stack of papers and return between 8:30 and 9:00 pm, at that time they would deduct the papers you had not sold from what you owed them, there were four daily papers at the time the Chicago Tribune, Chicago Sun-Times, Chicago American and the Chicago Daily News, they were sold at seven cents each and I earned two cents for each paper that I sold. Every day after school during the 7th and 8th grade both in the summer and in the winter while all of the other kids went home I went to the Tribune Loading Docks I now knew everybody down there the drivers the bums and the bosses in the circulation office (I even became friends with some of the printers), each night I would be taken to my newsstand by one of the drivers in the winter time it was freezing and I couldn't wait for the night to end I was so cold my toes would be frozen, but I was making money and that allowed me to be independent of the mess at home and that was all that really mattered.

In December of 1968 I was in the 8th Grade going to school every day and working my news stand every night, my dad had become very ill but it is hard to tell the difference between drunk and sick so I did not notice at first. He was still going to work each night but by the end of the first week of December he was so sick he could not go to work and that Wednesday I came home from school for lunch and he was waiting for a taxicab to go to the hospital. I told him that I wanted to go with him and he said no, that I was to stay here with Florence who was passed out drunk on the couch, at the time he gave me all of the money he had on him hugged me and said "I'm sorry, but you're going to have the same type of Christmas that you had five years ago" and then he left. That night I did go the newsstand and I was very troubled by the unknown. The next day I did not go to School (I did not return to school until after the funeral) I went to the Cook County

Hospital where he had been admitted to try and find out what the hell was going on and when he would be home.

They would not let me go upstairs to see my father because I was underage. I told the Cook County Sheriff Deputy my situation and he was kind enough to have the nurse come down to speak with me, she told me that he had advanced TB in both lungs and he was in a coma. They were going to transfer him to the Municipal TB Sanitarium at Pulaski Road and Peterson on Friday, there was nothing more I could do so I went home. Florence spent the next week drunk on the couch just getting up long enough to go to the liquor store for more whiskey. She was also pissing all over herself and it smelled bad in the living room. I did not return to School or the News Stand and on Monday when I came home from the store Florence was sitting up on the couch and said "Your father is dead!

Now what the hell are you going to do?", a brief moment of panic set, I just felt numb for a moment, then I recovered and called the TB Sanitarium to get more details and they informed me that he was in fact still alive but still in a Coma. What Florence did was very cruel and changed my opinion of her forever. Tuesday morning the sanitarium called me with good news my dad was out from the coma and eating and talking, and then on Wednesday Morning they called me back and told me that he had passed away and I needed to contact a funeral home to come and get his body.

One of my Dad's drinking buddies was Mr. Burke of Burke Sullivan Funeral Homes, my dad had all of his insurance papers in one envelope and I took them down to the Funeral Home and Mr. Burke said that he would take care of everything. The wake lasted two days and all of my dad's drinking buddies showed up to pay their respects. Everyone was handing me money and I kept running across the street to the hot dog stand to take breaks from receiving all of the mourners. Two girls from my class at Nash came, the school had taken up a collection for me and they gave me an envelope with $100.00 in it. One evening after everyone left I and I was alone in the chapel I opened the lid on the bottom half of the coffin, I will admit that I was surprised and a little shocked to see that he had no shoes just grey socks, I guess they don't bury people with shoes on. One of my Dad's friends slipped a half pint of Seagram's 7 whiskey in his jacket pocket along with a pack of pall malls, I retrieved the cigarettes but he still has the whiskey. During the wake there was another issue that was being discussed by everyone, basically me! I had a housing problem simply put I was about to have nowhere to live. I had no relatives to take me in. I was now alone in the world, so one of my father's bar friends Don Roach and his wife Marge took me in, after the funeral, they took me by my house to gather my clothes and pictures and papers, and then everything else got left behind furniture, TV, Florence etc.

Staying with Don and Marge was not going well she did not like me at all, I returned to running my news stand each evening after school coming in late every night and she did not approve of that or anything else that I did. I had effectively lost the freedom I had had when my dad was alive. I graduated from the 8th grade in the summer of 1969 it was to be the last public school graduation that I would Have. In August of 1969 I started the 9th Grade at Austin High School it had been an all-white school until that school year when they began bussing black students in and on my second week there race riots that broke out at the school. One day had to run my ass out of there because people were getting hurt big time in there. I got chased as I was running to the train station, when I got home I told Don and his wife what had happened. That night they thought I was asleep and I overheard Marge saying that if I stayed she was leaving. I got to thinking about that. Then I realized that they had just received my dad's life insurance of $2.000.00, they were now getting my monthly survivor benefits from Social Security, so what the hell did they need me for? The next day I skipped School and that night while Don and Marge were sleeping I stole all of the money in the house and took off never to return. Don and Marge continued to collect my Social Security until I was 18!

CHAPTER THREE

─◈◈◈─

Living On The Streets

Living on the street when you are only 14 years old is a pretty complicated and scary thing to do. You start out by living and learning as the old saying goes, and boy do you learn! I had spent a lot of time on the Chicago Tribune Loading Docks after school when I was running newsstands after school so I knew the landscape and this was very helpful. I knew that I could survive here. There were a lot of runaway kids down here working on newspaper trucks being paid by the drivers so information was easy to get. As a 14 year old kid living alone on the streets you learn very quickly that people that help you only want one of three things, cheap labor, companionship, or sex and sometimes all three and if you're going to survive you have to make all of these things work for you without losing control or getting hurt. To put it mildly you have to grow up very fast. I spent the first couple of nights sleeping on stacks of newspapers in a storage room. I would work all day on the trucks and the drivers would pay me three dollars a day. This would feed me and kept me in cigarettes. There was a priest at Holy Name Cathedral in downtown Chicago that would let street kids come upstairs in the rectory and take showers. What amazed me the most is that people you would never suspect were in reality sexual predators but I became a master at using these people to get what I needed. For a while I was sleeping in the doorway of the Peoples Gas Company on Wabash Ave. I had a friend who was the doorman at the Millionaires Club he was an old black man and a very good person, he never asked me what my situation was but I think he knew, he would give me food and had on occasion offered me money I took the food but never the money. I looked forward to talking with him in the evenings. This was a good person who had no hidden agenda and my only real friend in the entire world at the time. I will always remember him and be grateful for his friendship.

During the three months that I lived on the Streets of Chicago I learned so much about people about life and about the world we live in, I was working every day and sometimes every night, drivers would often fight over me because I was a good worker. I was living off of cheeseburgers and soda pop from the Billy Goat Inn on Lower Wacker Drive, along with the free coffee and donuts the Tribune had on the loading dock each evening for the news stand guys. Sometimes the drivers would buy me lunch but my biggest challenge was finding a safe place to sleep each night. For a while I was sleeping in the back of trucks at the Tribune Garage, quite often the trucks would leave in the middle of the night and I would have to wake up and jump out of the truck before I was detected and find another truck to sleep in. At the Chicago Sun-Times the Guard in the lobby would let you go up the escalator to the second floor lunchroom where the vending machines were, I started sleeping in the toilet stall at the end in the men's room, it was warm and it was safe nobody knew I was there and nobody bothered me. I would bounce back and forth between the Chicago Tribune and the Chicago Sun Times I was working for drivers at both Newspapers, I also spent nights in the Greyhound Bus Station I would find an empty ticket envelope and have it sticking out of my pocket so it looked like I was waiting for a bus. Once I was at the Train Station and I was hungry and a guy in a suit threw a little box of leftover chicken from his meal in the garbage, after he walked away I went and retrieved it and started eating the chicken. Apparently he saw me do that and he came over and yanked the box out of my hand, and then he gave me a five dollar bill and told me "Son, don't ever do that again! Ask someone for help if you're hungry" and he walked away, sometimes I think what kept me going were those extremely rare moments when you would come across good people but they were pretty rare. I did not work on the weekends so I would spend the entire day in the library. I had developed a thirst for knowledge and I satisfied this by reading books, I was actually home schooling myself. I loved to read and learn. On October 7, 1969 I turned 15 living on the street alone there was no party, no Happy Birthday wishes, in fact not one person in the entire world even knew that it was my birthday except me, I was truly alone and not one person anywhere cared, I was simply too busy surviving to think about that.

By December 1969 it was cold and snowy and street life was starting to take its toll on me. I was cold, hungry, dirty, angry and alone, and then on December 7, 1969 my life on the street suddenly and without warning ended. I had worked all day it was cold I had walked up to the Coffee Shop at Chicago Ave and Clark Street after having my coffee I had planned on sneaking into the Lawson YMCA Hotel to try and find an empty room that was open. While I was sitting at the counter drinking my coffee a heavy set middle age black man wearing a suit and overcoat walked in and ordered coffee to go, he kept looking at me and then he walked over to where I was sitting and asked "Are You Jessie Taylor?" and like a damn dummy I said "YES", that's when he showed me his badge and Identified himself as Detective Robert Lambkins with the Chicago Police Department Area Six Youth Division. Apparently there was a bulletin with my picture on it that had been put out by the Chicago Police Department. We left the coffee shop and walked to the 18th District Police Station which was about one block away, the youth office was on the second floor. When we arrived there he called Mr. & Mrs. Roach to inform them that I was in custody and they could come and get me. That was when things got confusing after they informed him that they did not wish to do so. I was no longer welcome to return to their home. The bottom line here was that they did not want me back, since they had already collected my dad's insurance money and were receiving my monthly Social Security Survivor Benefits (which they collected until I was 18 even though I was not there) they no longer needed me, I had served my purpose!

This created a situation for the Police, since I was only 15 they couldn't let me go (which was what I suggested that they do), so after making some phone calls the decision was made to send me to the Audy Home which was the City's Juvenile Correctional Facility. About an hour later two big cops came and took me down to the garage and put me in the paddy wagon. I was handcuffed at this point and off we went on a very bumpy ride to the Audy Home. It was about a twenty minute very bumpy ride, upon arrival they backed up to a walkway with a sign that said "INTAKE" as they took me out of the paddy wagon they removed my handcuffs, then had me empty my pockets and that's when they saw my cigarettes and matches, they told me to go ahead and smoke one last cigarette that it would be a while before I had another opportunity to do that again, so I sat on the tail gate of the paddy wagon and smoked my last cigarette, these two cops were actually good people.

CHAPTER FOUR

The Audy Home Chicago

The Audy Home was a Juvenile Correctional Facility a three story building that was opened in 1907. A turn of the century three story brick building located at Roosevelt and Cermak in Chicago. Directly across the street there was the Cook County Juvenile Court House. Both buildings were connected by an underground tunnel that travelled underneath Roosevelt Road. I spent the first three days in the intake unit, this is where you are evaluated and assigned a public defender. After this brief stay in the intake unit I was transferred to the third floor. All of the kids at the Audy Home were separated into different units by age group; each unit had a different T Shirt so everyone would know by looking at you what unit you were from. I was on unit 3-B and our T-Shirts had a Green Owl on the front; every one wore grey baggy pants that you were issued with your T-Shirt. The routine at the Audy Home was the same every day with the weekends being the worst. We got up every morning at 6 am and went to the TV Room (no talking allowed and you had to request permission to speak or to go to the bathroom and be escorted there and back), Breakfast at 7 am, then back to the TV Room, downstairs to the Classrooms at 9 am for School classes (in art class most kids drew court calendar's to keep track of their time and court dates as I did also), back to the TV Room at 11 am until lunch At 12 noon, back to the TV Room until 1 pm, then back down to the classroom until 3 pm, back to the TV room until Dinner at 5 pm, then to the basement gym for PT and back to the TV Room until bedtime at 9 pm. For punishment if any one misbehaved they would call you up to the front of the TV Room and make you bend over and slap you on your back really hard a couple of times, there were a lot of kids walking around with handprints on their back. At night we slept in an open dormitory a guard sat in a chair in the doorway all night, I slept next to the doorway and the guards would sit in that chair smoking cigarette's all night and I would lay there and try to inhale as much second hand smoke as I could. I had been to Court several times but it seemed that the Court system did not know what to do with me either so they just kept giving me new court dates.

Christmas day of 1969 at the Audy Home was much like any other day except that we got a visit from a guy dressed as Santa Claus. He was from the Salvation Army, he had a large bag of gift wrapped presents to give to everyone, they were all the same, a bottle of Aqua Velvet after shave and a bag of candy corn after he left the guards collected all of the after shave but let us keep the candy corn. The first week of January 1970 I had a new Court date. The procedure for going to court was they would handcuff you and walk you through the underground tunnel to the Court House and then handcuff you to a wooden bench in the waiting room outside of the Court Room until your name was called. The bench had a metal ashtray on each end and I was sitting next to a kid that had just been arrested and was brought in from the street,. This kid had cigarettes and matches so I bummed a smoke from him and sat there and smoked my first cigarette in a month. A short time later my name was called they undid my handcuffs, at which point I stood up and walked to the courtroom entrance and I took two steps into the Court Room and then everything went black, I fell flat on my face it was the rush from the cigarette that did me in that day so I got a new Court Date again. My Next and Final Court date was in the last week of January 1970 they had finally reached a decision as to what to do with me. I still remember the Judges words "It is the order of this Court that you Jessie Taylor a minor, and a ward of the State of Illinois, be transferred to the custody of the Illinois Department of Mental Health and be formally committed to the Chicago State Hospital!" that night I cried myself to sleep because I was scared of what was about to happen.

CHAPTER FIVE

The Chicago State Hospital

The Chicago State Hospital opened in the year 1869 as the Cook County Asylum for the Insane on 269 acres of land. The hospital was located on the far northwest side of Chicago. The name was later changed to the Cook County Institution at Dunning or Dunning Hospital for short. On July 1, 1912 the Cook County Board of Directors ordered all lands, buildings and equipment of the Cook County Institution at Dunning to be transferred to the State of Illinois and the name was formally changed to the Chicago State Hospital.

It is difficult to describe just how large this place was it was actually a city within a city. At one point in time 2,100 patients were housed there including unwanted children. It consisted of brick Cottage type buildings all were two story buildings with the exception of one four story building, the buildings were called Cottage Wards (CW). The Hospital was surrounded by an eight foot green wrought iron fence with pointed spikes at the top. I became very good at climbing over this fence. The main gate on Irving Park Road had a guard shack where hospital security was located, everyone coming in had to stop and be cleared by security to enter, they also patrolled the grounds 24 hours a day in white station wagons, responding to security issues in all of the wards, and they were the police department for the hospital.

When you first entered the grounds there was the Administration Building, a two story brick building that resembled a small town city hall building, there were winding asphalt paved roads that would take you to all of the other buildings on the grounds. The patient buildings were CW 1 Through CW 11, there was a retail store in a small one story brick building where you could purchase cigarettes, snacks, candy, soda pop etc., there was a Church with a steeple, a large building that was the kitchen that cooked the meals for the entire hospital and delivered them to the units by truck, a powerhouse and another building that held the boiler, these buildings had a smoke stack that was made of brick and stood 65 feet tall. There was also a three story modern fully equipped hospital with an operating room and emergency room, which also had its own ambulance. They also had a Firehouse with two fire trucks that was staffed with firemen around the clock; it was a completely self-contained city independent of the outside world. They even had a 20 acre cemetery where 38,000 people had been buried including some victims of the 1871 Chicago Fire; no new burials had been done there since 1920.

I left the Audy home on January 27, 1970, I was 15 years old. I was taken from unit 3-B thru the tunnel (this time with no handcuffs) to the Juvenile Court building, then outside where a white State of Illinois van was waiting. I had no idea what was waiting for me. When we arrived at the Chicago State Hospital I was surprised at how big this place was, it almost appeared to be a small city. I was brought to the Men's Receiving unit and I knew that this was a bad sign, I still remember sitting in the nurses' station during my intake interview, I was told that I was the only minor on the unit and I should behave accordingly, by this time in my life I was pretty much accustomed to bad situations and nothing either frightened me or really bothered me at that point. After the interview I was simply told to go to the day room. I walked down the hall toward the day room on my left was a large dining room, I still remember my first meal just like the Audy home you only get a spoon to eat with, next to the dining room was a quiet room which is a small room with nothing but a bed and a Plexiglas window in the door so they can observe you, on my right were two dormitory's with about 10 beds each. I saw several men secured to metal frame beds with leather restraints. When I entered the day room I finally saw something that made me happy, in the middle of the room there was a round table with chairs and on that table was a large can of bugler tobacco and rolling papers, yes the State of Illinois provided free smoking materials for those that could not afford to purchase smokes. I immediately sat down and rolled myself a cigarette, as I sat there smoking and thinking, I realized that once again I was in a situation of having to contemplate on just what the fuck I was going to do now. I got up and looked around at the room which was full of men watching T.V., playing cards, none of them looked like they were crazy. I went down the hall to the dormitory and found myself an empty bed, I got some linen a pillow and a towel from the nurse and claimed a bed, there was a stairway to nowhere half way between the nurses' station and the day room, and I walked upstairs to find a locked door on a dark landing with a lot of yelling and screaming on the other side of the door, I would later learn that the 2nd floor was the women's receiving unit, but the landing was dark, secluded, and no one could see me so that is where I started hanging out. Once I got to thinking about it this was not so bad, I had a bed to sleep in, I was out of the elements and warm, three meals a day, free smoking materials, and a hot shower every day, I could kick back and take my time in figuring out what I needed to do, after about three week's I came to the conclusion that as comfortable as I was I did not like being locked up! Now I needed to figure a way to escape, that was about the time that another kid arrived on the Men's

Receiving unit, he was a light skinned black kid he was 15 years old just like I was, his name was Willy I gave him the grand tour and told him everything I had learned since I arrived. There were only a few patients on the unit that were actually crazy; all the others had signed themselves in simply to take a vacation from life (at least according to them). Willy agreed that we needed to find a way out, in our quest to escape we discovered that the metal frame windows were severely rusted in the corners, and with a metal spoon from the dining room we took turns over a two week period working on those corners. Nobody paid much attention to us during that time, it appeared as if we were just looking out the window, we got it to the point that we were pretty sure that if we hit that window with a day room chair it would collapse out word and land on the ground in the snow. We still had one major problem, they had taken our clothes away, and we were wearing hospital gowns and slippers. Willy felt that if we could find a church, they would give us a set of clothes and bus fare to get us downtown. I thought about this for a moment and figured that surely God would be on our side, and since I did not have a better plan we would have to go with that one. The next morning with all the patients watching T.V., playing cards or otherwise distracted we took that window out with a day room chair and went out thru the opening that was left landing in the snow outside. Dressed only in hospital gown and slippers we ran across the service road in the snow to the perimeter fence which was a ten foot high green wrought iron fence with sharp points on the top, we both made it over and landed back in to free society. At this point we high tailed it to the closest ally, and we stuck to the alleys until we found a Catholic Church. We went up to the Rectory and rang the bell, a few minutes later an elderly priest opened the door, we were about half frozen to death at this point, we explained to him that we were in a lot of trouble and needed clothes and carfare to get downtown. He seemed to be very kind, and escorted us to a reception area in the rectory where he brought us each a cup of hot chocolate, we gratefully drank our hot chocolate while he went to find us a set of cloths (or at least that's what we were led to believe). When he returned he was accompanied by two uniformed Chicago Police Officers, we knew that we'd been had, after all I had been through I knew better then to believe or trust anyone or anything, however, up until that moment the church was still somewhat of an exception to that rule. This priest had just terminated that exception for me. Our moment of freedom had ended as suddenly as it had begun, what happened next is still a fond memory in my mind that will remain for as long as I live. We were escorted out of the church by the police wearing only our hospital gowns and slippers being escorted to the Chicago Police paddy wagon that was waiting in the church parking lot, the catholic grade school let out for recess and we suddenly were surrounded by what looked like 30 or 40 kids all chanting over and over "LET THEM GO, LET THEM GO, LET THEM GO, LET THEM GO"!

Both the police and the priest appeared to become very uncomfortable. I just smiled, I will never be able to forgive that priest for the trick he pulled on us, but those kids will forever have hero status in my mind. We were turned over to hospital security at the front gate, they put us in their white station wagon and drove us back to the men's receiving unit, we were placed in leather restraints for 24 hours as punishment for taking out that window and escaping. We were also heavily sedated, which I actually found helpful, the next day I saw that they had boarded the window up with plywood and it made me smile, about a week later I managed to steal a set of clothes, get the plywood off, and away I went this time alone. I walked downtown about 85 blocks, to my old haunt the Chicago Tribune loading docks. Then I managed to get myself sent out to a news stand and made $7.00 that night, I slept in a doorway downtown that night. It was pretty cold and I had been spoiled by the last few months of living inside sleeping in a bed and I knew that I was going to have to come up with a better solution. The next day I got on a bus and showed up on the doorstep of my childhood friend Bill. His parents let me stay there while I worked the newsstands every night, but after about three week's I guess they got tired of me. One day a Chicago police paddy wagon showed up and returned me to the Chicago State Hospital, even trusting people that I knew and trusted was not working out for me, but I was still learning. About a week after my return I was brought across the hall to a courtroom and formally declared insane "Patient is unable to function outside of a hospital setting" is how they put it, and committed to the Chicago State Hospital by a judge, the State of Illinois stated that I was unable to function outside of a State Hospital setting, and to this day I do not understand how they came to that conclusion. Shortly after the kangaroo court hearing, two people came to interview me, they were from the adolescent unit. They claimed that they were very concerned with my behavior on the Men's Receiving unit. I informed them that I was very concerned with the fact that I was only 15 years old and on the Men's Receiving unit. I also informed them that as long as I continue to be a patient on this adult unit against my will, that they should not expect any changes in my behavior. A few days later both me and Willy were transferred to the adolescent unit CW 10. This was a two story cottage type building there were two cottages connected on the outside by a concrete open porch with a small basketball court, and on the inside by a community dining room. The door to the dining room on each side was locked except for meals and evening snack time at 8:00 pm each night they served the same thing, buttered toast with cinnamon, sugar and milk. Sometimes I still make this at night for a snack. CW-10 was the boy's unit and CW-11 was the girls unit. This was in fact a locked ward that required a staff member to let you in and out. You entered into a small foyer on the left there was a record player, and a milk crate full of records on the floor that anyone could use, on the right there was a small hallway that had a Doctor's office where they held sick call each morning on weekdays. There was a large doorway that entered into the dayroom where on the left you had a wall mounted TV, a bunch of chairs, along with empty #10 food cans on the floor for ashtrays, on the right was a Ping-Pong table and a large open bathroom with six sinks and toilet stalls without doors. In the back of the dayroom was a large open area where group therapy and house meetings were held, on the right was a completely enclosed office cubicle surrounded by Plexiglas and a door the staff would lock themselves in this area if a fight broke or other trouble occurred, it was effectively their safe room. They would then call and wait for security. There was also another small hallways with small rooms just on the right hand side the first room was the Medication Room (there were many times when the keys for this room were stolen and we all had free drugs for a brief time). We were given Mellaril or Thorazine three times day (neither of these two anti-psychotic drugs is currently approved for minors). The next two rooms were quiet rooms which were small rooms with a bed and a locked door with a small Plexiglas viewing window. This room was used for discipline! They would give you an injection of a powerful drug that would incapacitate you, and then they would strap you to the bed with cloth or leather restraints and leave you locked in this quiet room. Then they would bring you meals at meal times. I spent a lot of time in these rooms. When I arrived I had only one set of clothes and they put in a request to the clothing room and I ended up with a whole wardrobe of cloths. This was a much better place than men's receiving there was about 25 kids on each unit. Every night at 9:00 pm they would open the door to go upstairs, we each had an open cubicle with a bed and a locker. There was only one mental health worker that worked at night, he was a bonified hippy, and one of the coolest people I have ever me. His wife worked at night on the girl's side. We would set in the office at night and he would tell all kinds of stories, he used to tell us how him and his wife would shower together to save water. Every morning we had to put all the chairs from the TV area together in a circle for group therapy, which was pretty much a daily bitch session. Based on how we behaved we would get points. If you had enough points you would get a grounds pass that allowed to come and go as you pleased. Next door was a three story school building, it was a combination grade school and high school, if you were not on restriction and had a grounds pass then you were allowed to go to school otherwise you were no. It was not a real school the Illinois Department of Education has no official record of this school ever existing, my favorite class was wood shop. They also had activities on Thursday evening they had a cooking class you could sign up for, there was a three bedroom home on the grounds that was once the home of the hospital administrator which was no longer being used and we would go there for cooking class, a lady that taught the class would bring all of the ingredient's and help us cook them, then we would have a wonderful meal. They had just opened a new facility across the street called the Chicago-Read Zone Center it was brand new, on Friday nights we would go there and watch a movie, they also had a swimming pool and we went swimming. The first summer I was there they took us (both units girls and boys) on a camping trip for four days to the White Pines State Park about a hundred miles from Chicago. They loaded us up on a big yellow school bus that had "ILLINOIS DEPARTMENT OF MENTAL HEALTH" in big black letters on both sides, nobody was real happy about that, and believe it or not they still passed out meds three times a day while we were there.

The Camping trip was great, for the first time in a long while I was happy and secure I had a girlfriend now her name was Debbie. We would eat together at the same table and we had sex in the stairwell of the school several times we were inseparable. While I was at the state hospital some of my upper teeth had rotted away from lack of dental care, the hospitals dental clinic pulled most of my upper teeth and I did not get a partial plate. A girl from my old neighborhood showed up on CW II one day. I was surprised to see her there, she looked pretty depressed. In the months to come her mother would always bring me something when she visited her daughter it was the only visitor that I got while I was at the Chicago State Hospital. One day I was outside returning from the school building and she was on the porch crying, this big kid from my unit was calling her names and yelling profanities at her, so I picked up a chair and hit him with it twice, after that I beat the hell out of him and off to the quiet room into restraints I went, but he got the message to my surprise she never spoke to me again, and what was even worse her mom stopped bringing me stuff, go figure! This was how you kept from becoming a victim,

you had to show everyone that you would
fight and that you would hurt them and then
they left you alone. When I turned 16 they
drove me to the Social Security Office to get
a Social Security Number. After that I got a
job in the Hospitals electronic shop paying
fifty cents an hour and yes they took taxes
out. A short time before my 17th birthday one
of the kids turned 18, now I had been under
the impression that when we turned 18 they
would let us go, out into the world and leave
us alone maybe help us get on our feet; this
did not happen he was transferred to an adult
unit. This told me that it was time to get the
hell out of here, I was very angry and scared
and these two things are the ingredients for a
very mean young man. I stole a wallet from an
adult patient on the hospital grounds. Back
then all ID's were just a piece of cardboard
without photos, I altered these ID's in art
class making myself 19 years old. I was ready
I had a plan I just prayed that it would work.

Each week I received $5.00 from my trust fund to this day I have no Idea where that money came from, this money allowed me to buy my cigarettes and other incidentals. The day I received my money I had decided that was the day I would be leaving the Chicago State Hospital and sadly Debbie behind. That morning after receiving my money they let me out to go to School and over the fence I went, hopped on a bus and went to the Illinois Department of Public Aid (Welfare) Office on the near South Side of Chicago.

CHAPTER SIX

Life On The Road

I arrived at the welfare office and stood in line at the intake window and when it was my turn I presented my art project the fake I.D.'s and to my surprise and relief they worked, I was told to have a seat until my name was called, well there was about 100 people already doing that so I joined them. Three hours later they called my name and I sat down with a case worker, I proceeded to give her a sob story and she approved me for benefits. On her typewriter she typed up a payment voucher and told me to take it to the window which I did and two hours later they called my name. I went to the window and they gave me a check for $93.00 which I took to the Currency Exchange across the street and cashed, knowing I had to get the hell out of town I grabbed a Taxi Cab and told him that I needed to go to two places. First I had him drive me to my friend Bill's house, why I did that I will never know outside of the fact that they betrayed my trust; and sent me back to rot in the State Hospital. Maybe I wanted to show them that shit was not going to happen. After we left Bill's house I had him take me to Midway Airport on the south side of Chicago. At the airport bought a ticket on Delta Airlines for $40.00 to Memphis, TN and away I went putting lots of distance between me and the Chicago State Hospital. I had about $28.00 left when I arrived in Memphis and after getting a cheeseburger fries and a coke that night I got beaten up and robbed, now I had nothing and I was not feeling so well I ended up checking into a mission and each morning I signed up for work and they sent me to different restaurants as a dishwasher/pot washer. After a week I had a little over $80.00 on me and I hit the road hitchhiking to Little Rock, AR, when I got to Little Rock I went to the Greyhound Bus Station and bought a ticket to West Helena, AR yes I was going home to a home that did not exist.

The Greyhound Bus stop in West Helena was at the little grocery store next to the house we had owned on north 2nd Street, they remembered me and were very happy to see me. I told them that my father had passed away and I was just here visiting. I walked up to the highway by the Tastee Freeze and rented a room at the Motel using my real name I had been using the name on the ID's I had stolen to get work in Memphis and I wanted to go back to being me.

Word spread pretty fast that I was back in town, after I got settled in my room at the motel I walked back to take a look at the home that had given me so many happy memories, by the time I got there Lisa and her parents were waiting in their front yard for me and they invited me to dinner. Lisa was in High School now and she had grown up to be a very pretty young lady, they asked a lot of questions that I did not have answers for so I just made stuff up. I spent the next couple of days walking around town visiting with people including Mrs. Lee my former school teacher. After spending two nights at the motel I was now forced to face the fact that my stay in West Helena was not sustainable, not only could I not afford to rent another night at the motel I did not have enough money left to buy a bus ticket to leave town. Yes, I was screwed and I knew it and I did not have a plan. I walked around the hill to Helena which was about a mile and a half, as the sun went down that evening I was sitting on the steps of the courthouse. I planned to just sit there all night and try to develop a plan in the morning. I must of fell asleep at some point because when I woke up it was dark, and I was freezing so I went in the little gangway on the side of the courthouse and laid down on the ground next to the window air-conditioner for the Sheriff's office, the heat the heat from the air exhaust felt very good and I quickly went back to sleep, They must of seen me because I was arrested several hours later and placed in a jail cell in the basement of the courthouse.

I spent three days in that cell without being fed, mainly because I do not believe anyone did any paperwork on my arrest, and no one knew that I was there. On evening of my second day they put a drunk they had arrested in my cell and he said that his wife would be there in the morning to see him, the next morning his wife was let in the cell to visit him. She had brought two tomato sandwiches and he gave me one, I asked his wife to go upstairs to the courthouse and tell the judge that I was down here and she did, three hours later the Sheriff himself came down and got me.

They had ordered out and got me a plate of food, they never did explain to me what had happened, and they had made some phone calls around town to find out if anyone knew me. Apparently Mrs. Lee is one of the people that they called she was now retired and had some influence with the town council. It seems that they all wanted to help me leave town. The Sheriff drove me to the town's orphanage where arrangements had been made for me to stay; there it was a large ranch style house with about eight boys on one side, and the same amount of girls on the other. Mrs. Lee and the county Judge had arraigned for me to go into the Job Corps. the only catch was that they required a complete physical, so the town paid for me to spend the night in the local Hospital on top of the hill to get the physical, once that was done I had to wait for about a two weeks for the paper work to go through.

During those two weeks of waiting I had a lot of free time; I hitchhiked around the twin cities. One day I was picked up by a rambler station wagon and not paying attention I just jumped in and sat down then the car took off, when I looked at the driver he was wearing a mask, fake glasses, and nose, and a fake mustache. Well, I bailed right out of there while the car was still moving got, some scratches and bruises from that, no big thing. I have no Idea what was going on there but I keep my mouth shut, things were going to well to create any drama. I had one last thing that I needed to do before I left town. I needed to be older with my own name on the ID, so I went downtown Helena to the Selective Service Office and told the lady I was 19, I appeared to be nervous and I apologized for not registering when I had turned 18. These were the days before computers and all records were paper records kept in file cabinets, no agency had the ability to verify what you told them, they would simply believe you. She was a nice lady and she sat down and typed up the paper work and the draft card and handed it to me. I had gotten what I needed. The day finally came for me to go to the Job Corps in Hot Springs, Arkansas they put me on a bus and wished me well.

CHAPTER SEVEN

The Job Corps/United States Navy

The Job Corp was created by President Johnson's Administrations War on Poverty in 1964. Designed by Sargent Shriver, and modeled after the depression era Civilian Conservation Corps (CCC). Their mission was to help young people between the ages of 16 to 24 receive their GED, along with vocational training and certifications in the construction trade, it was a work camp in the middle of the woods.

I was going to school in the morning and working in the afternoon living in a open bay barracks, this was not working for me at all, I believe that my biggest problem was the organized structure and following orders, these were things I was not good at. On my third week there I took the little money they had given me, a few clothes and headed through the woods to the highway, and began hitchhiking my way back to Chicago. I got as far as Bloomington, Illinois and got picked up by a Navy Recruiter, after hearing his sales pitch about joining the Navy, it sounded better than anything I had going so I pulled out my draft card and said "I'M IN!", he sent me to Chicago where I spent the night in a hotel and then went to the Armed Forces Examination and Entry Station the next day, after filling out forms and getting another physical, they said "your our boy!". I was sworn in, put on a plane, and sent to boot camp in Orlando, Florida.

Boot Camp was not so bad, but by the last week of boot camp they discovered that I was only 17, I was put into the brig for thirty days, now that was an interesting place we were in a cage that had bunk beds on one side, and exercise bikes on the other they would make us work out from morning to evening each day, we were marched to and from the chow hall for meals we wore the navy work uniform with a large yellow "P" for prisoner so everyone knew who we were. I was stuck in there for thirty days!

Once I was released from the brig I was sent to separations, where three weeks later I received a General Discharge under Honorable Conditions for Erroneous Enlistment. After going to Disneyland with my final paycheck from the Navy which had just opened I hit the road again. Once again I was homeless, this time I had money in my pocket.

CHAPTER EIGHT

On The Road Again

Not long after I left Orlando I turned 18 on the open road. I no longer had to lie about my age, but by this time I had created so many stories that I no longer knew what the truth really was. Each day I would head for the next large city getting maps from gas stations and truck stops, I became an expert at reading road maps. In each city I would stay in missions or Salvation Army Transient Lodges doing day labor in restaurants and factories, I travelled with a few carnivals, worked on a farm for a while; my objective was always to get the next big city each day. That did not always happen, sometimes I got dropped off at night in the middle of nowhere, in the pitch dark, and yes I was frightened, I would just sit there until daylight. I ended up hitchhiking all the way up to Colorado, now hitchhiking was illegal in Colorado and they were very serious about that. I spent thirty days in jail in Pueblo County for Hitchhiking, just outside of Colorado Springs. When I was released, and not wanting anymore free room and board from the county, I did the only safe thing, I decided that I would go onto the Interstate and walk to Nebraska or die trying, fortunately that didn't happen I got picked up by a truck driver and he took me all the way into Omaha. That night I got a bed in the mission and the next morning I signed up for work; they sent me out to a truck stop to wash dishes. I worked the 7 to 3 shift, then the 2nd shift dishwasher called in sick so I worked the 3 to 11 shift, then they needed a pots and pan man so I worked the 11 to 7 shift. When I got paid the next morning I went straight to the greyhound bus station. I was told that I did not have enough money to get to Chicago, so I bought a ticket to Rockford,

Illinois which is about 85 miles from Chicago. We arrived in Rockford at about 2am, and I had moved all the way to the back of the bus hoping the driver would not notice me, well he did a head count and had one passenger too many "ME"! He walked down the aisle and asked everyone to see their ticket I must have looked like I was about to cry when he got to me. I showed him my ticket the driver looked to be in his late fifties and he looked at me and asked me: "where I was trying to get to son? "And I told him "Chicago!" he looked at me for a moment as if he was trying to make a decision on what to do, he then told me that I would have to pay $11.00 more, I informed him that I had no more money, to which he replied "Son, I don't want to hear a peep out of you until we get to Chicago, do you understand me?" to which I replied "YES SIR!" and he turned around went back to the front of the bus and off we went to Chicago, Illinois. When we arrived in Chicago I walked around downtown for a while. I was 18 years old a legal adult no one could touch me, and I was back in my element, in the city that I knew like the back of my hand and that felt good.

I needed a place to stay so that evening I headed to the Pacific Garden Mission on State Street.

CHAPTER NINE

Return To Chicago

The Pacific Garden Mission opened on South State Street in downtown Chicago in 1923, at that time the area was called "Murderer's Row" because of all the people that were being killed there. By the time I arrived that had all calmed down it was simply known as skid row. Next door was a game arcade and an adult bookstore was Wilson Jones College Prep High School stands today. This was the homeless shelter for men of that time; in order to stay there you had to attend a church service each evening to get a bed ticket, then after the service everyone would go upstairs in a long line, you had to strip naked and give your clothes to the attendant who would then put them in a de-lice chamber that had a bunch of heat lamps, then they would give you a gown and a towel, after taking a mandatory shower the floor attendant would provide you with sheets and a blanket. On nights when it was cold outside I would lay in bed afraid to go to sleep. I was so warm and comfortable I just wanted to enjoy this feeling, if I fell asleep morning would come so quickly and I would be back out on the street freezing my ass off. Each morning I would sign up for work, they would send me out to various restaurant's downtown to wash dishes. The Pacific Garden Mission was a pretty big place it was divided into two sections on one side was the mission/homeless shelter, and the other side was the Servicemen's Center that provided safe haven and a free place to spend the night for military personnel that were traveling, mainly used by Navy Recruits that had just graduated boot camp in Great Lakes just outside of Chicago. The two sides were separated by a free medical clinic, soon after I arrived at the mission I was interviewed by one of the Christian counselors and given the opportunity to come into their program, this is where you live there and work for room and board and a few dollars a week called a grant. I figured that this would be better than having to show up every night for a bed. I was a very good worker, not long after I entered the program I became the night janitorial supervisor. They moved me out of the large dormitory over to the small dorm in the Servicemen's center, this was much more comfortable, I enjoyed talking to the military servicemen that passed thru the center. The staff and management at the Pacific Garden Mission were all very god people they really did care for everyone there. However, you always had to keep in mind that this was a pretty rough place; you would see things every day that reminded of this. I had carved out a very comfortable place for myself here, but I started thinking about wanting a real job and my own place to live. The problem was that I was so comfortable at the mission that I did not want to leave. Then it happened one night, I had went to the hot dog stand to get a hot dog and a coke before work I only had a dollar, so I bought my meal. Each night the Chicago Police cleaned State Street of homeless people, at that time they still had the vagrancy law on the books, if you did not have a least a dollar on you they could arrest you and put you in jail, as I was eating my hot dog a police paddy wagon pulled up out front and two cops came in and asked everyone to see their dollar. Damn, I had just spent mine, so into the wagon and jail I went. Not only did I miss work that night. I did not return to the mission because I was spending the night in jail, which meant I was no longer in the program. When I was released the next morning I took the paperwork they gave me and went to the welfare office. I checked in at the intake office using my real name this time and waited for almost 6 hours before they called me. I was promptly informed that they no longer gave you money or approved you on the same day. The process was now far more complicated, she did give me a letter to take to the Northmere Hotel on Chicago's far North Side that said my application was being processed, according to the caseworker they were very good about letting people stay there until they were approved for benefits. I thanked here, took the bus tokens she had given me, and headed off to the North Side thinking that once again somebody up there must like me.

CHAPTER TEN

The Northmere Hotel

When I think back I would have to say that the Northmere Hotel was the best and worst thing that ever happened to me. When I first arrived at the hotel I showed my letter to the desk clerk and he called the manager, moments later she came down the hall into the lobby she was a very heavy set middle age lady, maybe 350lbs with blonde hair, her name was Mary Ann but everybody called her mom. The Northmere Hotel was the city's dumping grounds for everyone that no one else wanted, a destination of last resort, and Mary Ann was the manager on a lifelong mission to save everyone she could, anyway she could and that was her downfall in the end. The hotel was a six story turn of the century brick building with 160 rooms. Each floor had six rooms with a private bath four at four at the other end, and the other twelve rooms had adjoining baths with a shower that you shared with the person next door.

I gave her my letter from public aid and she read the letter and then she looked at me like she was trying to make a decision. I must have been a site I had spent the previous night in jail my hair was a mess I was exhausted and I was waiting for her to tell me that she could not help me, to my shock and surprise she looked at the desk clerk and said "put him in room 204 for the time being" then she turned around and went back to her apartment on the first floor.

The desk clerk gave me the key to room 204 and showed me where the stairs were next to the large TV room off of the lobby. There were two elevators the one at the front of the hallway was manually operated and was for staff use only; they used this elevator for garbage collection each evening and to respond to trouble on the floors. The residents consisted of alcoholics, drug addicts, senior citizens, and mental patients all in one building. The second elevator was the passenger elevator for use by the residents, it was a very old elevator with a heavy metal door and a gate, these were both turn of the century elevators that still required machine rooms on the roof. My room was at the front of the hallway around the corner in a short hallway. This room consisted of a single bed with an institutional mattress, a dresser with a mirror, a chair, and a window, the bathroom was just a toilet and a shower that I shared with the person next door. I had my own room and this was the Hilton Hotel for me I just wondered how long it would last. There was a clean towel on the dresser I did not have any soap but I took a shower anyway and went right to sleep.

The next morning I woke up and I was hungry, I had not eat anything the day before and I had no money, but I would deal with that later, so I got dressed and went downstairs. The lobby was packed with residents waiting in line at the desk. Mary Ann was passing out money and having them sign for it. She held most of the resident's money for them, and she would give them between three and seven dollars each day depending how much money they had on the books. I went into the TV room and sat down trying to figure out where to go for a free meal, when everyone had received their money and left, the desk clerk came into the TV room and told me "Mary Ann wants to see you at the desk" well I figured this is where I get my walking papers at least I got a good night's sleep. I got up and went to the desk where Mary Ann stood with a stack of one dollar bills in her hand and she asked me "Do you have money to eat?" and I told her "No!" She gave me three dollars and had me sign for it, and told me to come to the front desk every morning and she would continue to give me money to eat until I got my check. I wanted a cheeseburger and a coke but I needed cigarettes so I got smokes, two cans of pork & beans and I stole a small box of plastic spoons from the corner store and returned to my room.

The Northmere Hotel was owned by two very successful business men Mike and Sam, they also owned five other similar hotels in Chicago and they were not in the charity business, each room needed to be paid for each month. Talking to other residents I learned as much as I could, also that other people were being carried by Mary Ann and given money to eat each day because they had no income. They too were waiting for their benefits to be approved. Some had applied to the Illinois Department of Public Aid some to Social Security, now this was back when A medical diagnosis of Alcoholism qualified you for Social Security Disability Benefits (President Ronald Regan put an end to that in 1980). If you were waiting for Social Security, Public Aid would give you a monthly benefit and would deduct it from your retroactive pay when you were approved.

Now I was skeptical about everything at this point in my life, and I was very troubled by the fact that she was letting me and others live here for free and give us money that we did not have on the books each day. Where in the hell did she get the money to cover all of this? I would later learn that she stole it. Just about every month residents would die at the hotel or in the hospital but their checks would continue to come and Mary Ann would continue to cash them and pay rent on their rooms, and these rooms were used to take people without money or anywhere else to go. She would use what was left over for whatever she needed to use it for, that's how she did it and had been doing this for years. To her credit she helped a lot of people doing this including me not to say that this was right and in the end justice did prevail.

Sitting in my room that evening I realized that I had two cans of pork & beans and no can opener, I went downstairs to Mary Ann's apartment which consisted of five connecting rooms, with the kitchen door always being open. Every member of the hotel, staff lived at the hotel and Mary Ann's kitchen was open to them 24 hours a day. The door was always open they were like one big family, I could smell the food cooking and it smelled so good I wished I was part of this little family they had going but I was not. I only wanted to ask them if they would be nice enough to open my can of beans and they did so I went back upstairs to eat my dinner. Over the next couple of days I walked up and down

Argyle Street asking every business owner if they needed help they did not, I needed a job but had no carfare to go and look for one so I was limited to employers that I could walk to. Each morning I would get my three dollars and my beans and go downstairs to ask someone to open them, the fourth night that I did this Mary Ann was there alone. She invited me into her dining room and asked me "How are you doing? "I told her about my job search and she asked me if I would like to work in a hospital, I replied sure I would be happy to work anywhere. She told me that she had a connection that I should wait a couple of days to see what she could do. She added that I should come down each night and tell who ever was in the kitchen that she said I could eat there. That night I had my first hot meal in a week and it was good. Life was getting better but I was very concerned about how long that was going to continue. One week later Mary Ann told me that I had a Job interview in the morning, the next day she would drive me to Northeast Community Hospital, and that I would be interviewed for the position of orderly I was very excited.

The hotel only used one Ambulance Service which was Aaron Ambulance, and everybody went to the same hospital which was Northeast Community Hospital. The hotel had a medical clinic on the first floor, and doctors from northeast came there each week to see patients. Everybody had welfare medical cards that paid for their visits. When we arrived at the hospital we did not go to human resources, we went to the hospital administrator's office in the executive suite of the hospital. The hospital took up the space of three storefronts on Clark Street and was a seven story building. I did not know it at the time but I had already been hired the visit was just a formality; I was told that I would need a white shirt, white pants, and white shoes when I reported to work. I filled out the application and the W-2's and then Mary Ann took me to a department store and bought me everything that I needed for work. She was truly a remarkable and wonderful person. I would later learn that these were favors that would have be returned on demand. A week later I received a letter from Public Aid informing me that my application for benefits had been denied! They claimed I was eligible for a different benefit and I could not collect both but they did not say what it was, as far as I was concerned I had a job now and didn't need them so it was not important.

I loved working at the hospital it was exciting and different every day. It was my first real job! I was on split shifts; mainly my job was on the patient wards the nurses were wonderful. They taught me how to take blood pressures, and temperatures. At the beginning and end of the shift I would take and log everyone's vitals, make beds, assist with baths, serve meals, etc., in the evening I had an extra duty should someone die usually on the geriatric floor, I would have to prep the body and take it to the morgue in the basement. This was done by tying their hands and feet together, filling out a toe tag with their name, age, date and time of death, wrapping them in a white plastic sheet and tying it off at the neck, waist and feet place the body on a cart and taking it to the basement. The morgue had a stainless steel refrigeration unit that had a metal shelve behind a 10 foot long stainless steel door. You could fit two bodies side by side on it, a couple of times it was full and we had to stack bodies on top of each other. I also got to work in the emergency room on occasion, I liked being there and learned a lot about life and medicine when I worked in the E.R. I had been working at the hospital for about six weeks when I returned to the hotel and was told that Mary Ann wanted to see me. When I went to her apartment she told me that I had a phone call from a caseworker with the Illinois Department of Children and Family Services. My first thought was" Oh' hell no! I want nothing to do with these people, they had already fucked my life up enough" but she convinced me to call the number. I called the next day and was told by the caseworker that he would give me an appointment to come into the office, to which I replied "That is not

 ever going to happen! I have a job, I have a place to live, I am 18 years old now just leave me alone!" to which the caseworker responded "OK son, I have looked at your file and believe me I do not want to meet you anymore than you want to meet me, but I have a job to do! I am willing to do this on your terms, give me a date and a time and a place and I will buy you lunch." I was off that

Thursday and we met at a hotdog place on Sheridan and Montrose.

At the time the Illinois Department of Children and Family Services (DCFS) was a fairly new agency. On the day we met at the hot dog place I was in informed that even though I was 18, I was still a ward of the state of Illinois until I turned 21. The State of Illinois was still my parents and responsible for me. The caseworker made me a proposition that I could not refuse. They would give me $296.00 a month with a green card for medical and dental, no visits with my caseworker would be required in return all that I had to do was stay out of trouble, I could also keep my job, it would not matter WOW! I accepted on the spot, I now had a 2nd job that would pay me to stay out of trouble. I could do that (I hoped). I continued to work at the hospital. I used my medical card to get a partial plate denture; I was also helping out at the hotel.

I had moved to a room on the first floor with a private bath, I was working the desk at night and on my days off and responding to whatever emergencies happened on the floors fights, fires, etc. I was probably on the payroll there and never new it with my check going to Mary Ann. I started working the night shift at the hospital and the night nurse had me passing medication and giving injections which resulted in a hospital investigation. I was asked to provide a written statement which I refused to give and was promptly fired. I started working for the hotel full time no paychecks Mary Ann would simply give me money for whatever I needed. She was also telling everyone that I was her son! I was one of the few people she trusted so on the first of the month she would send me to the post office to pick up everyone's checks, with 160 residents the post office did not deliver the hotels mail it was held at the will call window and we went to get it. I was the only one she trusted on the first and the third when the checks came in, after she had the residents sign the checks, she would sign all of the dead people's checks and then she would put them in a large envelope and I would take them to the currency exchange. The guy there would add them all up take his cut, and give me a large envelope with the cash in it. I would take this back to Mary Ann I would make sometimes two or three trips doing this. There was so much cash that nobody could keep track and I was slipping a little out too. By this point I was drinking a lot and doing a lot of drugs and buying pills from hotel residents. We would find bodies in rooms and I would get their cash from their pockets, if I did not take it somebody else would have. I can assure you that they would not have got to the funeral home with their money. I turned 19 at the Northmere Hotel and I was a basket case by this time. The State of Illinois had just lowered the drinking age to 19 so now

I was going to the bars. There was violence everywhere, I had witnessed a murder at the hotel and this got me to thinking. Maybe it was time to get the hell out of here. I went to the Illinois National Guard after seeing an ad in the paper and joined, they sent me to Basic Combat Training at Ft. Polk, LA and after eight weeks me and the Army came to the mutual conclusion that we incompatible. I was promptly discharged for insubordination. Back to the Hotel I went broken and defeated. Shortly after returning I was sitting in my room one night drinking vodka and decided that life had beat me so I took an entire bottle of 750mg Placidol Sleeping pills. Someone must have found me because I woke up in the I.C.U at Ravenswood Hospital. From there I went to the psych unit where I spent a week pulling myself back together. After returning to the hotel I got a job at a factory and continued to help out on my free time over the next year and a half I went through five different jobs, while also working at the hotel, my drinking was what kept me sane because I was surrounded by insanity, to the point that one night I got a call to go and check a garbage odor on the 6ᵗʰ floor so I went to the front desk to get the pass keys for the 6ᵗʰ floor. There were six long chains hanging at the desk, each chain held all of the keys for each floor, when I got to the 6ᵗʰ floor I quickly determined what room the odor was coming from. I found the key and opened the door and what I saw and smelled was horrible! Lying there on the bed was a white guy who had turned black and had swelled up and exploded! They said he had been dead for maybe six weeks! I threw up and slammed the door shut, when the police arrived they had me go to the store and get five cans of coffee. We had to evacuate the entire floor due to the odor. I poured coffee grounds in the room and the hallway to absorb the odor. Not long after that I found a new job around the corner from the hotel as a commercial engraver and decided to leave the Northmere. I rented a small apartment next door to where I was working, Mary Ann was not happy about this but in my mind it was time to go. In my apartment at night I was completely alone and started to miss the hotel. I began drinking a lot I was only making $1.60 an hour at work and I was no dummy my future was not bright. One night while I was drinking a pint of whiskey the phone rang, the problem with that was I had not had the phone turned on! When I answered it no one was there but when I hung up and picked the receiver up I got a dial tone, so I called the phone company and when I gave them the number they told me that number was disconnected! I told them that was the number I was calling them from, so they had someone come out and disconnect the line. About two weeks later I went to the Navy recruiter and joined the Navy again, this was probably my last chance to make something of myself and I knew it I would not fail this time. It also turned out to be a good thing on another front, the building I was living in burned down in the middle of the night while I was in boot camp!

CHAPTER ELEVEN

The United States
Navy Submarine Service

I arrived at the United States Navy Recruit Training Command on February 3, 1976. I completed boot camp went to "A" School in San Diego, CA. While I was in "A" school I volunteered for the Submarine Service, after meeting all of the qualifications, and graduating in the top ten percent of my "A" school class (which was one of the requirements) I received orders to the United States Navy Submarine School in Groton, CT. After graduating from Sub School I arrived at my first Submarine, the USS Mariano G Vallejo SSBN 658. I qualified Submarines in eight months and earned my Dolphins. In 1978 I was burned with first and second degree burns over 14% of my body while on patrol in the north Atlantic. Shortly after the accident in 1979 I was transferred to another Submarine the USS Sunfish SSN 649 a fast attack Submarine that was in the ship yard at Pascagoula, Mississippi. By this time my drinking was so out of control that I was sent to a Alcohol Treatment center at the U.S. Navy Seabee base in Gulfport, MS. I never completed the treatment program because the area was hit by Hurricane Frederick. I was sent back to become part of the skeleton crew on the Submarine for damage control during the hurricane. We were beaten up pretty bad by the first part of the hurricane and during the eye the CO decided to sink the Submarine at the pier which we did. The next morning we had no way to bring the Submarine to the Surface, and since the cranes had been blown over on their sides we had to wait for them to upright a crane to pull us back up. For the next two weeks we lived in a barracks that had no roof and about an inch of water on the floor, and then we were moved into apartments the Navy had rented. I left the Navy with an Honorable Discharge in April of 1980, having nowhere else to go I returned to the Northmere Hotel in Chicago.

CHAPTER TWELVE

After The Navy

After returning to Chicago I held many different jobs and was in and out of a lot of mental health facilities and alcohol treatment centers, I finally left the Northmere Hotel for the last time in 1983; I did not want to die there. Not long after I left the hotel they were raided by a multitude of Federal, State, and local Law Enforcement Agencies Mary Ann was arrested and charged wi many counts of forging U.S. Treasury Checks and State Welfare Checks. I met my wife in 1984 and a couple of months later I was arrested by the United States Secret Service, after providing them with my handwriting samples and since I had not forged any checks,(I was just the runner) I was allowed to provide a written statement as to my involvement after receiving Immunity from prosecution by the United States Attorney I did that and was released.

I married my wife in 1984, and we went on to have three wonderful children, the next five years were the happiest times of my entire life, I was stable, held a good job, had a great family life, I was finally loved and a part of a real family.

This also ended in divorce; I am currently retired living in Tampa, Florida and have a good relationship with my children.

WEBSITES OF INTEREST

http://law.justia.com/cases/federal/
appellate-courts/F2/771/292/379966/

http://bulk.resource.org/courts.gov/c/
F2/771/771.F2d.292.85-1083.html

http://news.google.com/newspapers?nid=25
06&dat=19771203&id=VIJJAAAAIBAJ&
sjid=wwsNAAAAIBAJ&pg=3774,986792

ABOUT THE AUTHOR

J. Taylor has realized his lifelong quest of telling a story that he felt needed to be told. It is the Author's intention to show in detail what happen's to a child once that child is placed in state custody. J. Taylor is the father of three adult children all U.S. Army Veterans that have served in Iraq and Afghanistan, he is currently retired and resides in Tampa, Florida.